The Deep Ocean

Contents

What to Do

YOU MIGHT NEED:
- a dictionary
- a thesaurus
- an atlas

NOW:
- choose a face
- when you see your face, you are the leader
- when you are the leader, follow these steps:

1. Predict

Say to your group:
"I think this page is going to be about..."

You can use these things to help you:
- photographs
- captions
- headings
- what you already know

Tell your group to read the page silently.

2. Clarify

When your group has finished reading, ask them if there is anything they don't understand.
Say: *"Is there anything anyone doesn't understand?"*

It could be: • a word
              • something someone has read

3. Ask Questions

Ask your group if anyone would like to ask a question about what they have read.
Say: *"Does anyone have a question they would like to ask?"*

4. Summarize

Now... you can tell your group what the main ideas are on this page.
Say: *"I think this page has been about..."*

The World Beneath the Sea

I predict this is going to be about...

Deep under the oceans is a world of wide plains, deep valleys, and high mountains. There are plains wider and mountains higher than any found on dry land. In fact, the world's longest mountain range, the Mid-Atlantic Ridge, is under the sea.

The world under the oceans is a very cold and dark place, and because venturing there is such a challenge, much of this fascinating world has never been explored by humans. It is actually easier to explore places such as the moon or Mars than to explore the depths of the ocean. It is too dark for human eyes to see, and the crushing pressure of the water makes it a place where no human could survive. Yet this hasn't kept scientists from finding ways to explore this mysterious world and uncover many of its secrets.

Does anyone need to have anything clarified?

Mt. Everest is the highest mountain in the world. If this mountain were in the deep ocean, there would still be more than a mile of water covering it!

Does anyone have a question to ask?

My summary of what we have read is...

Why Explore the Deep Ocean?

I predict this is going to be about…

Exploring the deep ocean can help scientists learn about the life on our planet and its history. The deep ocean can give scientists information about how the continents formed, how earthquakes and volcanoes start, and how islands and mountains are made. Scientists can learn what life and Earth's climate were like billions of years ago.

This deep, dark world is teeming with fascinating life. Some of the species that live deep under the ocean existed in prehistoric times. We can learn a lot by studying these creatures and how they have adapted to live in such an extreme place. Many of the creatures that live on the ocean floor are very different from animals that live on dry land. What scientists can learn from these creatures helps us to understand better how life works.

Deep ocean sponges

Does anyone need to have anything clarified?

The deep sea can be as rich with life as a tropical rain forest!

STOP

When you read, "teeming with fascinating life," what picture do you get in your head?

 Does anyone have a question to ask?

 My summary of what we have read is...

Deep Ocean Explorers

Early Explorers on the HMS Challenger

I predict this is going to be about…

At first, scientists thought that no life existed in the deep ocean. Nothing was known about it at all. Then, in 1872 a ship called the HMS *Challenger* set off on a long and important journey to explore the world's oceans.

A key mission for the scientists on board was to gather as much information as they could about the deep ocean, and to prove that life really did exist there. These scientists were able to measure the depth of the water, map the bottom of the ocean, and discover its deepest sections. They measured the water temperature and collected samples of almost 4,000 new species of animal.

The scientists collected so much information, that it took fifty huge volumes to record it all. The information was so helpful that scientists used it for many years.

Does anyone need to have anything clarified?

The HMS *Challenger*

I predict this is going to be about...

It would not have been an easy task to gather information about the deep ocean. The scientists needed special equipment to measure, map, and collect samples. They used a dredge, or a trawl, that dragged across the seabed. They had winches that lowered and lifted ropes to measure how deep the ocean was and nets to catch ocean life. The nets were more than 30 feet wide and had 11,000 feet of rope! When they were pulled up, they were often torn and the wood was crushed because of the great water pressure. To measure the ocean's temperature, they used a thermometer, but the thermometer was small and hard to read. It was also affected by the water pressure, even though it was protected by a metal case.

Anything that the scientists took from the ocean was sorted, preserved in special bottles, and carefully labeled.

Does anyone need to have anything clarified?

An early submarine

Early diving equipment

11

I predict this is going to be about…

While scientists could gather some information about the deep ocean, they couldn't go down and see it for themselves. No protective suit could prevent a person from being squashed to death under the great weight of water. Getting humans into the deep ocean was a huge challenge. Then, scientists William Beebe and Otis Barton invented a steel chamber called a bathysphere and made the first trips into the deep ocean.

The bathysphere was attached to a ship by a long cable. It had a porthole and a telephone so that the scientists could talk to those above about what they were seeing. However, it was extremely risky. These adventurers did not know if they would freeze to death, or if the bathysphere would stay watertight so deep under the water. The cable could have cut the air hose, and they would have been without oxygen. Yet they did succeed and traveled deeper than anyone had been before.

Does anyone need to have anything clarified?

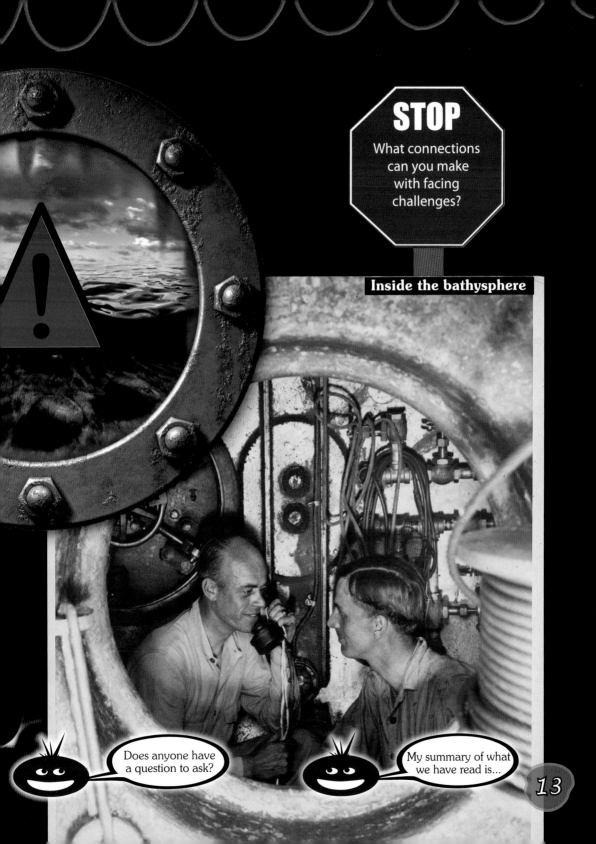

STOP
What connections can you make with facing challenges?

Inside the bathysphere

Exploring the Deep Ocean Today

Using Submersibles

I predict this is going to be about...

Today, scientists are able to learn a lot more about the ocean floor because of deep-sea submersibles.

A submersible needs a ship to launch it and pick it up again, because it has a limited power supply.

The first submersible was called *Alvin*. It had small, thick portholes to see out of. Submersibles have special lights to penetrate the total darkness of the deep ocean. They have video cameras and robotic arms to pick up samples such as life-forms, rocks, and water. The samples are stored in a basket on the front of the submersible.

However, while submersibles can descend very deep, some parts of the ocean are too deep even for them.

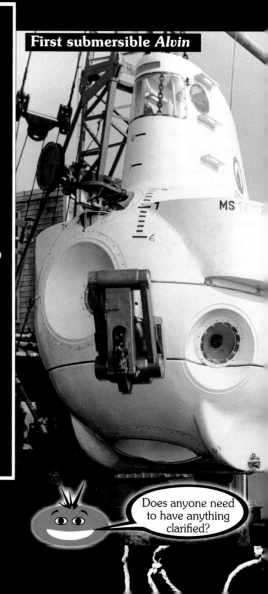

First submersible *Alvin*

Does anyone need to have anything clarified?

Preparing a submarine to explore the deep ocean

Does anyone have a question to ask?

My summary of what we have read is...

15

I predict this is going to be about...

Scientists also use satellites and robots to study the deep ocean. From high above the Earth, satellites constantly record information about the deep ocean. A satellite's instruments can measure the colors in the ocean, which can tell scientists about the depth of the water, water temperatures, and even about microscopic creatures that live in the water. Back on Earth, people study this information to see how water currents and temperatures change, and to get clues about weather patterns that affect the whole planet.

Robots, which are sometimes called "ROVs," are useful for exploring the deep ocean. They have lasers that measure the size of fish, and arms that grab tiny samples off the ocean floor. They can also be used to track fish, providing information about how they live.

Does anyone need to have anything clarified?

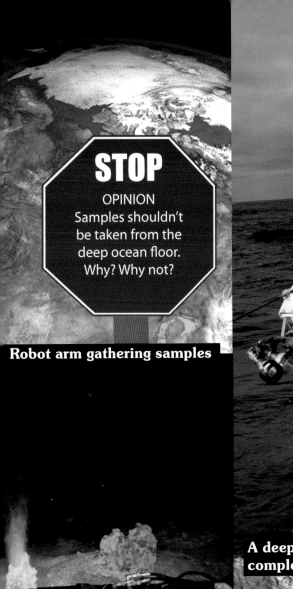

STOP

OPINION
Samples shouldn't
be taken from the
deep ocean floor.
Why? Why not?

Robot arm gathering samples

A deep-sea robot completes its mission.

Does anyone have a question to ask?

My summary of what we have read is...

Hot Spots

I predict this is going to be about…

In the darkest, coldest places of the ocean floor, there are some of the most active volcanic areas on the planet. There are erupting underwater volcanoes, and incredible hydrothermal, or "hot," vents.

In a hydrothermal vent, very hot water comes out of an opening deep on the seafloor near volcanoes. The water from the vents contains minerals and even at times precious metals. Sometimes, the water spewing out of the vents is black because of these minerals and metals. The minerals can fall out of the water next to the vents, creating huge chimneys.

Even though the chemicals spewed out by these vents are extremely hot and poisonous, scientists have discovered many different species of plants and animals living here. In fact, there is life in this extreme place that exists nowhere else on Earth. The giant tube worm is just one example. It is an amazing creature with no mouth and no stomach!

STOP

When you read, "water spewing out of the vents," what picture do you get in your head?

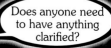

Does anyone need to have anything clarified?

Life survives deep under the ocean.

An underwater geyser

More Creatures of the Deep

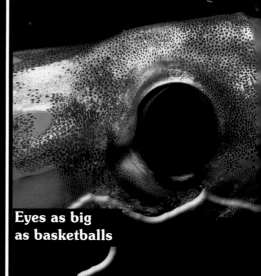

I predict this is going to be about...

Thousands of bizarre creatures live their lives in the deepest, darkest ocean, rarely seen by humans. These fascinating creatures have adapted to their hostile environment. Some are jelly-like and have soft bones, helping them to cope with the water pressure. Others have large mouths, long pointed teeth, and stretchy stomachs so that they can swallow their prey whole. Some, such as the anglerfish, even have their own lights to help them find prey!

Because there is not much food in these deep waters, the creatures that live there must survive on what floats down from above or eat each other.

One fantastic creature that lives in the deep ocean is the giant squid. It has eyes as big as basketballs, probably the biggest eyes of any living creature. It is not a sea monster, but some believe that legends of sea monsters may be based on this amazing creature!

Eyes as big as basketballs

Does anyone need to have anything clarified?

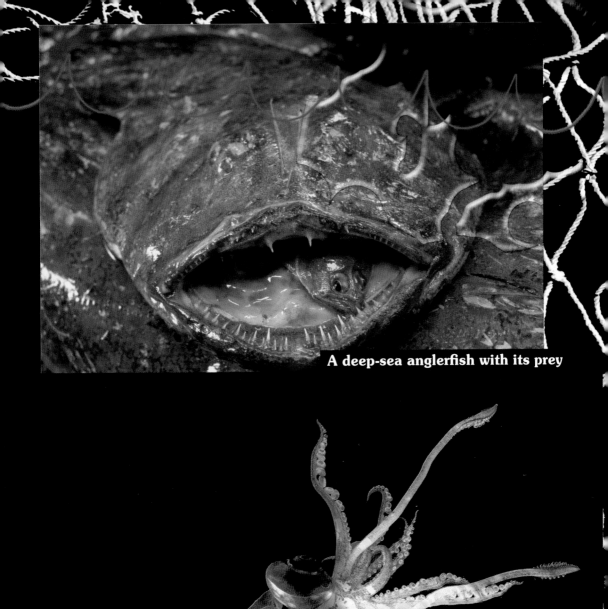

A deep-sea anglerfish with its prey

Sponges and Corals in the Deep Ocean

I predict this is going to be about…

Glass sponge

Sponges and corals might seem like plants, but they're not. They are actually animals – and some species can survive down in the deep ocean.

Most deep-sea sponges are brown or gray. They are slow growing, and some species have been living in the deep ocean for more than 600 million years.

Like the sponges, corals also grow slowly and can survive for hundreds – maybe even thousands – of years. They feed on microscopic creatures. Corals provide a home for many other animals in the deep ocean, rather like a rain forest does on land. Scientists think that corals may be the source of new medicines and could give clues to changes in our climate.

Does anyone need to have anything clarified?

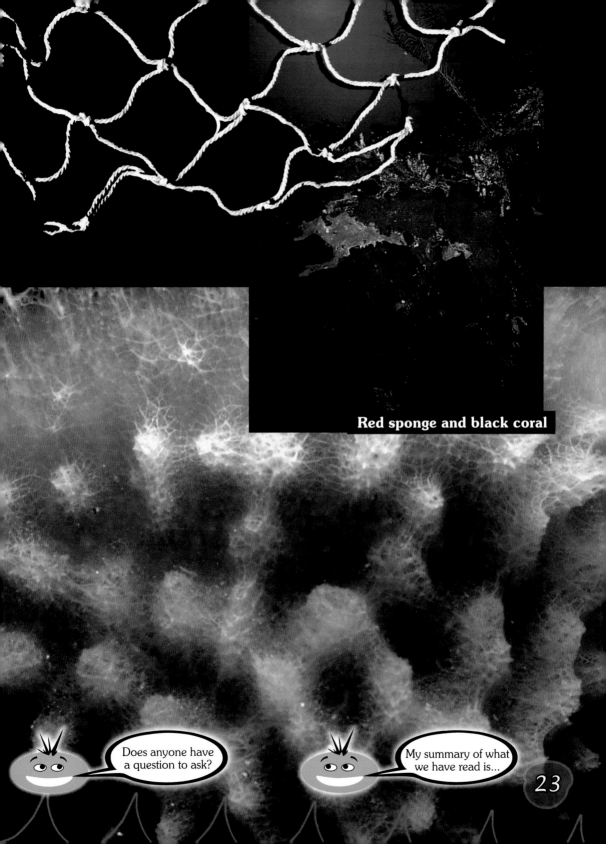

Red sponge and black coral

Damaging the Deep Ocean

I predict this is going to be about...

The world's deep oceans are very important for our survival on land, and we must protect them. Yet sadly, scientists exploring the deep ocean have found piles of garbage that people have dumped in the ocean and that has floated down to the ocean floor. If the junk on the seafloor was just household garbage, that would be serious enough, but people have dumped huge containers of poisonous waste here too. Everything that is dumped into the ocean will eventually find its way to the seafloor and do serious harm to all that lives there.

Deep ocean fishing called bottom trawling, where huge heavy nets are dragged along the seafloor, is another problem. These nets have rubber wheels and heavy plates that can crush everything they move over.

Sponges and corals can take hundreds of years to recover, and many have disappeared altogether.

Does anyone need to have anything clarified?

Dead sharks dumped back in the ocean

Garbage on the ocean floor

 Does anyone have a question to ask?

 My summary of what we have read is...

Protecting the Oceans

I predict this is going to be about…

It is vital that we care for and protect the fascinating world deep down in the ocean. Not only is it the world's largest environment, it has the biggest variety of life on Earth, and there is still so much to learn about it.

Some scientists think that if there is life on other planets, it could be similar to the creatures that live in the deep ocean. When scientists study how these creatures survive in such an extreme environment, it could help them find other places to search for life. It could also help make new advances in medicines and treating health problems.

The more that scientists can discover about the deep ocean, the more they will be able to understand the future of humans and planet Earth.

STOP

What connections can you make with trying to discover something?

Does anyone need to have anything clarified?

A deep-sea anglerfish

Something to Think About

ARGUMENT: All fishing in the deep ocean should be banned.

FOR

?

AGAINST

?

ARGUMENT: Robots shouldn't be used in the deep ocean.

FOR **?**

AGAINST **?**

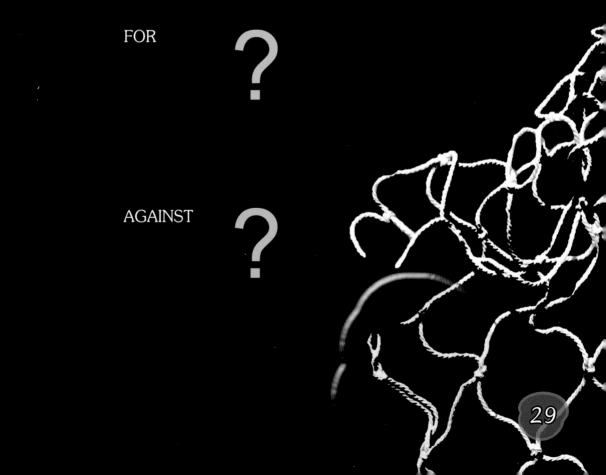

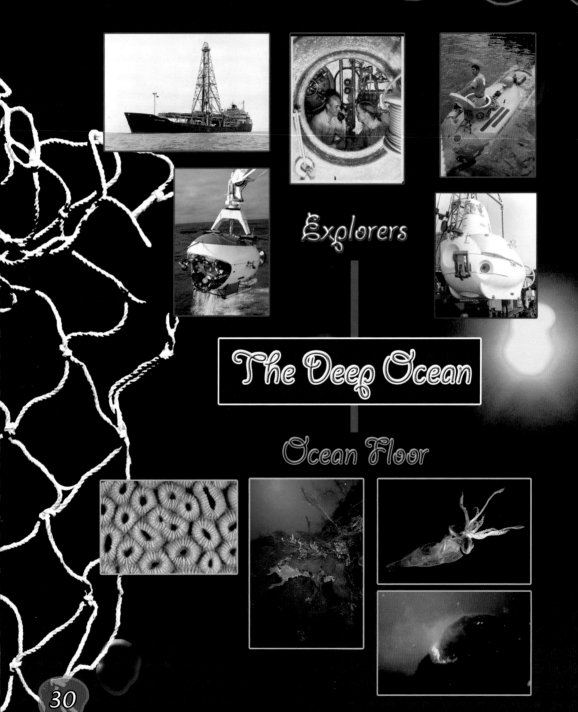

Explorers

The Deep Ocean

Ocean Floor

Want to Find Out More?

Try searching in books and on the Internet using these key words to help you:

bathysphere
deep-sea creatures
deep-sea exploration
deep-sea robots
deep-sea sponges
deep-sea submersibles
HMS *Challenger*
junk in the deep sea
underwater geysers

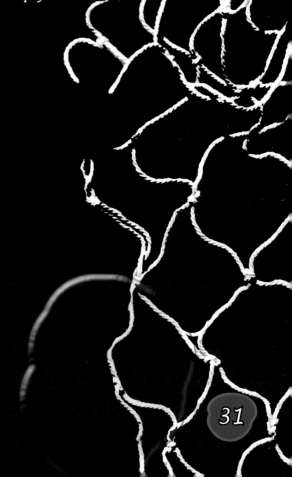

Index